America's Best
Fresh Water Fishing

Other Fishing Books By the Same Author

America's Best Fresh Water Fishing

By
Ray Ovington

Illustrated by the author

Maps by Moraima Ovington

JONATHAN DAVID PUBLISHERS, INC.
MIDDLE VILLAGE, NY 11379

Jonathan David Publishers, Inc.
68-22 Eliot Avenue
Middle Village, New York 11379

Library of Congress Cataloging in Publication Data

Ovington, Ray
America's best fresh water fishing.

1. Fishing—United States. 2. Fishes, Fresh-water—
United States. I. Title.
SH463.09   799.1'2'0973   77-24740
ISBN 0-8246-0219-6

Printed in the United States of America

Table of Contents

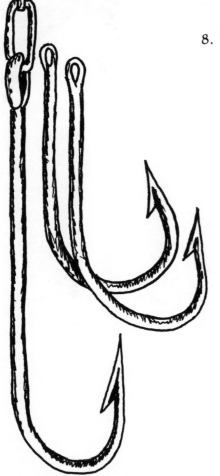

Acknowledgments

This is to offer my sincerest thanks to the many authorities on fishing and streams who have helped me over the years in compiling the data and information contained in this book. There are also many unknown anglers and local residents who have added to the treasury of information gathered here while the author was fishing the streams and states. Special thanks go to Duncan Campbell, who, after much urging, wrote the first book of its kind: *88 Top Trout Streams of the West*, plus of course my publishers: Alfred Knopf, Thomas Nelson, J.L. Pratt, Digest Books, Hawthorn Books, Little-Brown, Freshet Press, and to the editors of *Field & Stream*, *Sports Afield*, *True*, *Argosy*, *Saga*, *Outdoors* and *Pennsylvania Angler*, and the now defunct *New York World Telegram & Sun*.

Much appreciation goes to: Frank Amato, editor, *Salmon, Trout and Steelheader* magazine; Cyrus Brown, fishing guide, Caribou, Maine; E. Kliess Brown, Chief, Information and Education, Idaho Fish & Game Department; Virginia Buzek, fly tyer, Visalia, California; Angus Cameron, editor/sportsman, Wilton, Connecticut; Duncan Campbell, member, Orange County Fly Fishers, California; Paul Collier, member, Inglewood Fly Fishers, California; Bernard W. Corson, Director, New Hampshire Fish & Game Department; Harry Darbee, fly tyer, Roscoe, New York; Jim Deren, Anglers' Roost, New York City; Eli L. Dietsch, Supervising Aquatic Biologist, N.Y. State Department of Environmental Conservation; Richard G. Diggins, District 1 Fisheries Biologist, Vermont Fish & Game Department; William E. Easte, Assistant Aquatic Biologist, Massachusetts Division of Fish & Game; James Eriser, President, Federation of Fly Fishermen; Art Flick, fly tyer, Westkill, N.Y.; George Forrest, former editor, *Pennsylvania Angler*; Alvin Grove, Editor, *Trout*, Trout Unlimited; R.C. Holloway, Chief, Information and Education Division, Oregon Wildlife Commission; Willard T. Johns, Director, Pennsylvania Fish Commission; George A. Kaminski, Chief, Information & Education, Wyoming Game & Fish Department; Mark Kerridge, Vice-President, Federation of Fly Fishermen; Harry Kime, member, Orange County Fly Fishers, California; Tom Knight, Information Officer, Washington Department of Game; the late Larry Koller, angler, Neversink, New York; Don Leyden, angler, Holyoke, Massachusetts; Stanley Lloyd, a founder of Cal Trout, California; T.M. Lynch, Fish Manager, Colorado Division of Wildlife; G. W. McCammon, Chief, Inland Fisheries Branch,

California Department of Fish & Game; John McKean, Wildlife Director, Oregon Wildlife Commission; Jim Petersen, sportsman, Hartford, Connecticut; Martin H. Pfeiffer, Associate Aquatic Biologist, New York State Department of Environmental Conservation, U.S. Geological Survey Water Resources Invest. 8-73, Department of the Interior; Steve Raymond, editor *Flyfisher*, Federation of Fly Fishermen; Michael Riedell, officer of Cal Trout, California; Jack Samson, editor, *Field & Stream*; Ed Sens, fly tyer, Bronx, New York; Phillip Vallarine, member, Inglewood Fly Fishers, California; Cole W. Wilde, Chief, Connecticut Department of Environmental Protection; Dick Wolfe, Vice-President, Garcia Corp., N.J.; J.F. Yoder, Editor, *Pennsylvania Angler*.

Introduction

I've personally fished most of the waters written about in this book; some more often than others; some for a one-time-only try. I've come away from them amazed that the 48 contiguous states of America can offer such a variety, and in some cases, an unbelievably large amount of natural environment that still produces top-flight angling. In some instances the newer impoundments created by dams have added immeasurably to the store of angling prospects, even at the sacrifice of valuable streams.

In writing and compiling the facts in this book, I have, in addition to my personal notes, consulted many experts and particularly the conservation departments of the states in order to offer a more rounded appraisal of the waters described or referred to in the text. Some states are loaded with first class fishing and others are not.

The one main point I wish to make here is that this book is a collection of what I consider the best, most famous and *most consistently* productive waters that contain and produce the best catches of the biggest fish. In selecting specific waters I've asked myself: "Would I travel 500 miles to fish such-and-such lake when a really top lake is right in my home state or at least within an easier, shorter drive?" For example, there is some fairly good trout fishing in West Virginia, but would I go there in preference to a top Pennsylvania or New York State stream if I lived say, in Boston? The answer is, No.

Now, I fully realize that many readers might feel abused if I do not mention a specific lake or stream that they consider to be tops. I found it very difficult to eliminate some very good waters from the editorial stockpile, but, again, I have had to hold fast to my present specific guidelines. Some states are not included here, and some mentioned only briefly because they are not important in the context of this book.

In several instances, such as the Rangeley Lakes in Maine, the St. Lawrence River section of New York State, or a myriad of lakes and streams, say in Wyoming, I have referred to the AREA as being famous and tops rather than to mention twenty or more fishing "spots" in that area. A book that mentions all the waters leaves me in a confusion into which I don't want to lead you.

The state, stream, area and in-text maps will help you to recognize and locate the waters so you can readily reach them by car, and without confusion. Trout stream maps have labels of large block lettering with arrows pointing to the stream. Maps with lightly shaded areas indicate lakes and streams where other game fish besides trout are found. Where necessary and possible, I've given dependable information sources for more detailed up-to-the minute statements of prevailing fishing conditions. I've also not fallen too many times into the trap of relating a personal anecdote when writing about pet waters. Neither have I wanted to involve the how-to of fishing techniques. I assume the reader knows how to fish, or will avail himself of the needed research on fishing, boating, camping, hiking and RV travel. I've added an appendix to the book which covers most of these subjects in general. It also offers insights into the various fish species you'll be catching on "my" waters.

I've also written this book with the hope that all of us will grow to appreciate these waters, protect them and guard them from exploitation, destruction or pollution.

A Note On the Drawings

My good wife, Moraima, labored far into many nights drawing these maps. They are composites of maps supplied by guides, outfitters, conservation departments and private concerns. They are simplified as much as possible, but do contain enough direction for you to follow—right to the fishing area.

The decorative line drawings are by the author.

MAINE

The entire state of Maine is famous for its fishing. It is the symbol of wilderness and unshaven guides wearing plaid wool shirts, red caps and leather boots. For many years the traditional first salmon to be caught from Bangor Pool on the Penobscot River was sent to the President of the United States. Sportsmen from New York and other eastern cities made these waters famous for over a period of nearly a hundred years. Famous angling authors extolled the virtues of the Pine Tree State to add further fame to the area—a fame richly deserved.

From one end of the state to the other, it is true north country with timbered ridges, some very high (for the East) mountains and a landscape that seems to be more water than land—chains of lakes with winding, connecting streams.

I've fished most of the best midstate waters in the Sebago Lake Chain with its many streams just outside of Portland to the Rangeleys and toward the center of the state dominated by the state's largest lake, Moosehead Lake. While most good trouting is in the main ponds and lakes of this region, the connecting streams and lake feeder brooks produce well enough to supply many a camp dinner. The upper part of the state from Greenville on the southern shore of Moosehead clear up to Canada, Quebec on the west and New Brunswick on the north and east, is my favorite country. It may be true that some bigger trout can be had further south in the state, but I favor the north because of its absence of civilization and overdevelopment.

Maine is the home of the native brook trout, lake trout and landlocked salmon, and in a few remaining streams in the extreme northeast, the Atlantic salmon.

1

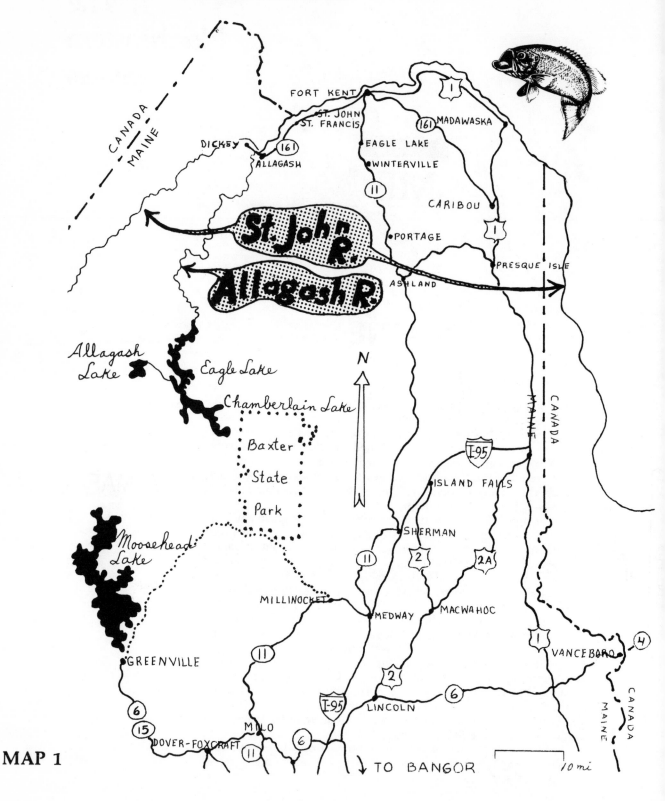

MAP 1

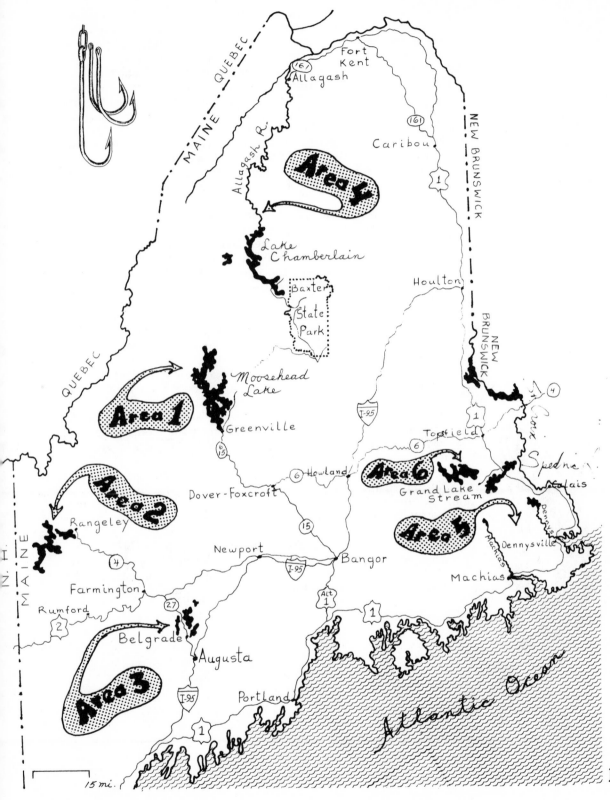

MAP 2

Part of the fishing flavor of this country is the background and atmosphere. Actually the trout are simply not as many or as big as they used to be. But it is famous country and it can produce for you some big ones if you are persistent.

My first encounter with Maine was when I was a boy. I'd like you to experience the trip my father and I took with two guides in canoes from Greenville, Maine. We paddled and portaged the entire run, some 450 miles up the lakes and through the Allagash (East Branch), which finally joins the St. Johns River along the New Brunswick border. From there we canoed all the way to the Bay of Fundy at the city of St. John. We had to rely on the trout, bass, perch and lake trout as staple diet. Even then the trout were small, with the exception of two 4-pounders I caught below a falls one evening.

The Allagash, then, is the epitome of what Maine has to offer, in my opinion.

Beginning in the headwater lakes of Allagash, Eagle and Chamberlain, the waterway is fed by hundreds of streams and broken by countless lakes and ponds all the way to the junction with the West Branch. There are public campgrounds all along its course, but most of it is miles from the nearest road.

Trouters educated on waters of Pennsylvania and the Catskills and even anglers from the West will have to discard some of their techniques when hunting for big brook trout in Maine. These fish have their own way of doing things, and I've been skunked trying to apply sophisticated casting and fly patterns that work well elsewhere. The conventional Down Easterner usually fishes with two or three wet flies on a leader, always the classic patterns, such as the Royal Coachman, Parmachene Belle, Black Gnat and Silver Doctor. You can catch the fish on others, but the traditionals usually produce. Short casts, long drifts are the techniques.

The best way to fish the Allagash is from a canoe, especially if you have to do any portaging.

This is blackfly country in May, June and into July, and the mosquitoes come along in June through the summer, so go equipped.

I should also recommend as famous and profitable the extreme eastern portion of the state, and also nearby portions that border New Hampshire as being tops especially for smallmouth bass as well as trout and salmon. Most of this, again, is wilderness

and the best waters are available by portage or flying in. There are many access roads into the privately owned timberlands, but these roads do not appear on commercial maps, since they are not maintained by the county or state. Get maps from the Maine Tourist Development Commission, Augusta, or from the lumber companies such as Brown, and International Paper Co. These are available at local chambers of commerce.

Basically, the fishing season opens when the ice goes out from the lakes, which happens about the middle of April in the lower portions of the state. This is the best time for landlocked salmon fishing if you intend to take them on the surface. When the water warms up, they go deep to hold company with the lake trout and big brook trout. The bass season is a summer proposition.

Late summer finds Atlantic salmon fishing in Maine's two very good reclaimed salmon rivers, the Dennys and the Machias, in the extreme northeastern section of the state. Extensive progress has been accomplished by joint efforts between New Brunswick and Maine to also develop the St. Croix watershed to again provide magnificent runs of Atlantic salmon as well as superb smallmouth bass and landlocked salmon-trout fishing. Fly fishing only is allowed on these waters.

Despite the fact that modern highways have made Maine quickly available to millions of tourists and sportsmen from the major cities of the East and guests from farther away by plane, the area has resisted overdevelopment, thanks, in large part, to the lumber and wood industries who owned major portions of the northern section. This has limited the hot-dog-stand era from entering and despoiling.

Unlike many other areas of the country, there are well-established information sources, and I list a few here.

For complete information on canoe outfitting and trips into the Pleasant Lake and Washington County wilderness waterways and the Grand Lake Chains, write Maine Wilderness Canoe Basin, Box F, Carroll, Maine, 04420.

In the Grand Lake Stream Area, write Weatherby's, Box F-74, Grand Lake Stream, Maine, 04637. Trout, bass, lake trout and salmon.

For Allagash canoe trips and fishing, write Greg Jalbert, P.O. Box 126, Ft. Kent, Maine, 04743.

For all species of game fish near Princeton, Maine, write Long Lake Camps, Princeton, Maine, 04668.

For famed China Lake, contact Nelson Bailey, China, Maine, 04926.

For information on Moosehead Lake area, write Moosehead Hotel, P.O. Box 235, Rockwood, Maine, 04478.

Since the State of Maine contains so many famed fishing areas, the reader will find it helpful to check the 6 areas below, for easy access.

Area 1. The best way to the Moosehead Lake region is by State Routes 6 and 15, north from Bangor to Greenville and Rockwood. There is also a scenic private road down from Baxter State Park.

Area 2. The Rangeley Lake area is best reached from State Route 4, northwest from Farmington.

Area 3. The Belgrades are easily reached by State Route 27 off Interstate 95, just north of Augusta.

Area 4. The Allagash River System is in a roadless area, with only two access points; one by a private road across Lake Chamberlain at the south end (coming out of Baxter State Park) and the other by State Routes 11 and 161 at the north, near the New Brunswick border.

Area 5. The Atlantic salmon rivers, the Machias and the Dennys, are located in the extreme eastern portion of the state. The stream is reached from Machias on U.S. 1 on the Atlantic Coast, and the Dennys about 25 miles further north along U.S. 1, at Dennysville.

Area 6. The Grand Lake Stream area is north and west of Calais. Rich in tradition for its trout, bass and landlocked salmon fishing, this area blends into the Spednic Lake area and the fabulous St. Croix River system, which also includes some Atlantic salmon fishing. Numerous resorts, guides and outfitters serve the region.

MAP 3

The
Northeastern
States

NEW HAMPSHIRE

Like the state of Maine, New Hampshire has varied fishing and fishing conditions. In the northern and central parts of the state, you'll find brown, rainbow, brook and lake trout, landlocked salmon, and smallmouth bass. Largemouths are in the south, however. The famed and most beautiful golden trout (not to be confused with the golden trout of California) is a prize worth going after, even just once! The golden is native to Lake Sunapee. Big Dan Hole Pond near Ossipee (which is near the Maine border) and Tewsbury Pond near Grafton, east of Lebanon, are also good spots for brown and brook trout.

The largest lake in the state is Lake Winnipesaukee in the center of the state in the famed "lakes region." It's crowded in vacation season. Brook trout, lake trout, bass and panfish are the fare.

Northern New Hampshire has good fishing all around. North of U.S. 2 are the Connecticut River lakes, including Back Lake and Lake Francis (formed by Murphy Dam from the headwaters of the Connecticut). Also in that area is the Connecticut River along U.S. 3 near Pittsburg, just below the dam at the junction of State Route 3 and U.S. 3. The river is good for many miles—all the way down to Stratford. Brown and rainbow trout abound.

The White Mountain zone south of U.S. 2 is excellent territory for bass and trout, and you can get the up-to-date facts from the publication, *Outdoors in the White Mountains*. This is available from White Mountains Region Associates, Lancaster, N.H. 03584. It lists 100 rivers and ponds. The best take-off point is at Woodsville, on U.S. 302, or Franconia Village on Interstate 93. This is gorgeous vacation country.

For further details write the Economic Division of Tourism, Concord, New Hampshire 03300.

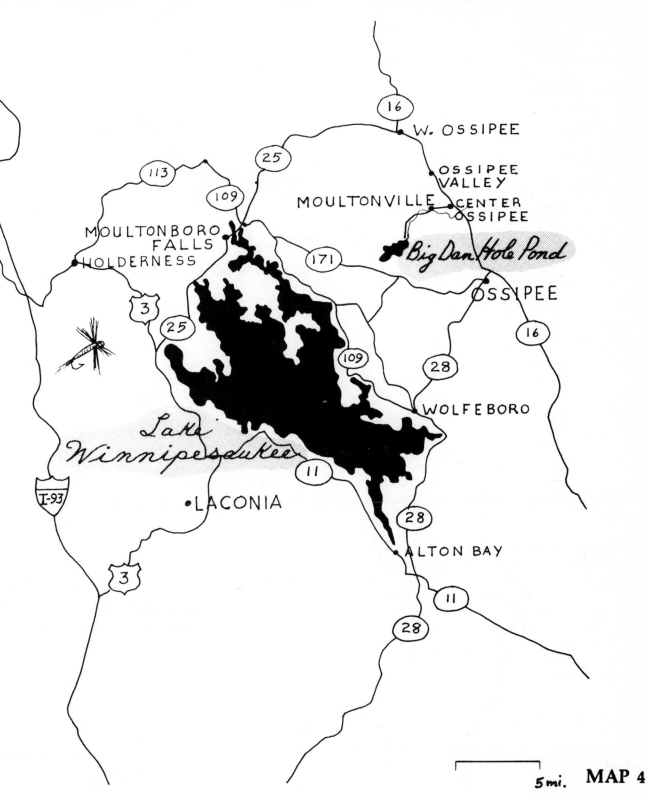

MAP 4

5 mi.

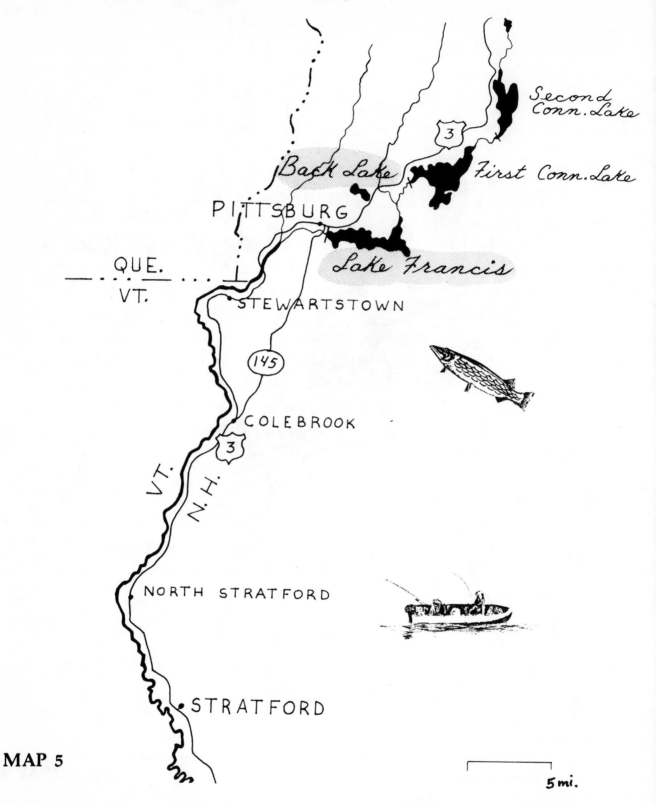

Second Conn. Lake

First Conn. Lake

3

Back Lake

PITTSBURG

QUE.
VT.

Lake Francis

STEWARTSTOWN

145

COLEBROOK

3

VT.

N.H.

NORTH STRATFORD

STRATFORD

MAP 5

5 mi.

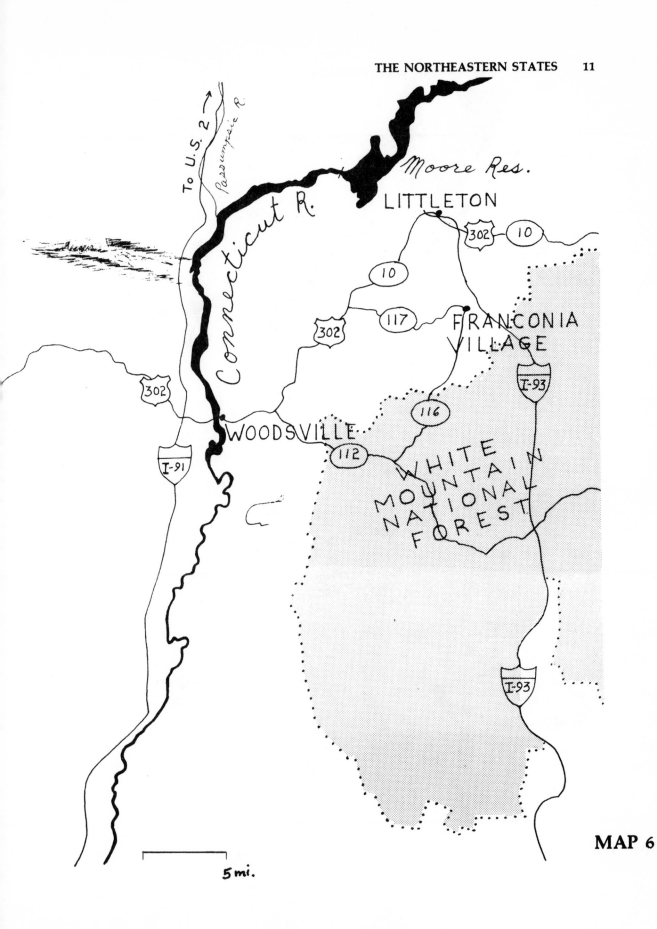

MAP 6

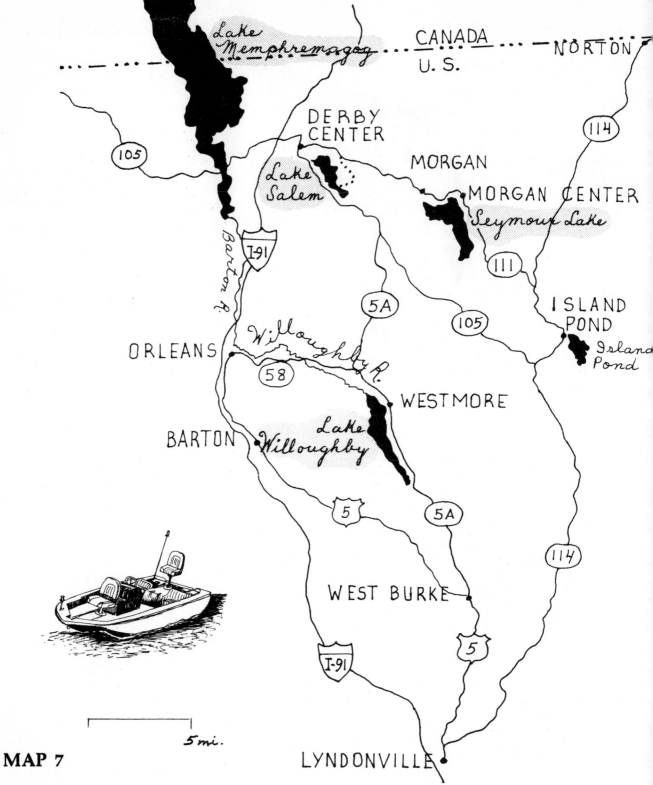

CANADA
U.S.

NORTON

Lake
Memphremagog

114

DERBY
CENTER

105

MORGAN

MORGAN CENTER

Lake
Salem

Seymour Lake

111

Barton R.

I-91

5A

105

ISLAND
POND

ORLEANS

Willoughby R.

Island
Pond

58

WESTMORE

BARTON

Lake
Willoughby

5

5A

114

WEST BURKE

5

5 mi.

I-91

MAP 7

LYNDONVILLE

VERMONT

The Granite State's eastern border is the Connecticut River. Lake Champlain covers 100 miles of the state's northwestern border and then flows south into Poultney River for another 50 or so. In between are the ever-gorgeous Green Mountains with their 4,000-foot elevations, clear, sparkling streams; small lakes and ponds. There are also the medium-sized streams where trout fishing is excellent-to-good in the upper reaches and some good bass fishing is found further downstream.

Vermont's Battenkill, the White, the Mad, the Lamoille and the Dog are among the best known for brook, brown and some rainbow trout.

Lake Champlain and Lake Memphremagog on the Quebec border are lake fishing bests for trout, landlocked salmon, lake trout, plus limited muskellunge, pike and walleye pike.

Fortunately for the hurried angler, Vermont is well networked with excellent roads despite its often rugged terrain. The best north-south route is Interstate 91 along the Connecticut River for most of the state. Interstate 89 crosses the northern section of the state from Burlington on Lake Champlain to Barre. U.S. 2 goes from Barre straight across the state to the New Hampshire border. In the south, U.S. 4 offers the same ready access from New York State to Rutland and so on to Lebanon, New Hampshire. U.S. 5 goes along the entire eastern section of the state.

Lakes Champlain and Memphremagog, and Willoughby, which is joined to Lake Memphremagog by the Willoughby and Barton Rivers, is one of the finest territories for both trout and smallmouth bass. Heavy lake trout are also taken up to 25 pounds or more. There is public fishing reachable at Westmore, on State Route 5 A, which is reached by coming north from the junction of State Route 5A with U.S. 5 at West Burke, or by coming east on State Route 58 from the junction with U.S. 5 at Orleans.

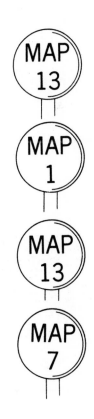

MAP 13

MAP 1

MAP 13

MAP 7

MAP 7

MAP 8

MAP 9

MAP 10

MAP 12

I've had good days on this one, and I caught the first lake trout of my career here.

Another top lake in the region is Seymour Lake, with some very good lake trout, landlocked salmon, rainbow, brook and brown trout plus a generous portion of smallmouth bass. Public fishing areas, boat launching sites and boat liveries are available at the town of Morgan Center on State Route 111, which can be reached easily from I-91 at Interchange #28, or north from Island Pond, also on State Route 111.

While you are there, try Lake Salem, near the town of Derby Center. There is a public fishing area at the end of a dirt road off State Route 111. The Salem Lake Camps are excellent for you and the family. They offer boats and guides. Landlocked salmon fishing is excellent in May, and you can also catch lake trout, bass and walleyes in the summer.

Quimby's Camp, a world-famous caterer to anglers, is on Averill Lake, also called Great Averill Pond, almost upon the Canadian border and reached by State Route 114.

One I've fished many times is Crystal Lake, a beauty spot that contains rainbows, lake trout, salmon and smallmouth bass. It is just west of Lake Willoughby on U.S. 5 at Barton. Take Interchange #25 off I-91 to Barton and Crystal Lake Park.

For your river fishing, the Connecticut River is the main waterway, and its tributaries offer very good angling for bass, trout and walleye the full length of the state. From my own experience, the Nulhegan River tributary is a beautiful run in wild timbered hills with rainbows and brook trout. State Route 105 from Bloomfield on the New Hampshire border to as far up as Island Pond on State Route 114 is good for bass and trout. An also-ran, for brook and brown trout, is the Moose River, one of the better tributaries of the Passumpsic River, entering the Connecticut River south of St. Johnsbury.

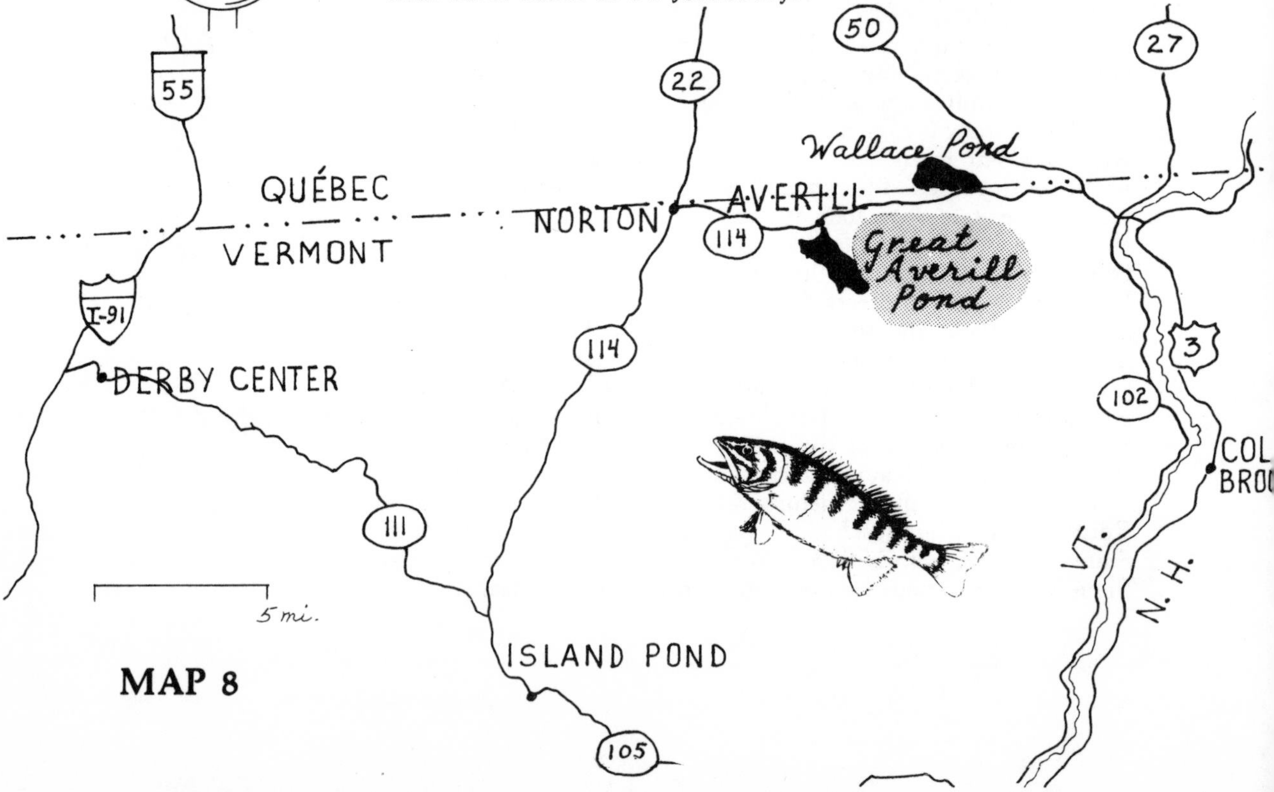

MAP 8